THE ENLIGHTENED HEART

THE
ENLIGHTENED
HEART

An Anthology of Sacred Poetry

Edited by Stephen Mitchell

1817

HARPER & ROW, PUBLISHERS

New York

Grand Rapids, Philadelphia, St. Louis, San Francisco
London, Singapore, Sydney, Tokyo, Toronto

Library of Congress
Catalog Card Number 89-45320
ISBN 0-06-016208-2

FIRST EDITION

Designer: David Bullen
Compositor: Wilsted & Taylor
This book is printed on acid-free paper.

92 93   10 9 8 7 6 5

To Zen Master Seung Sahn,
who taught me everything I don't know

CONTENTS

FOREWORD

"We dance round in a ring and suppose, / But the Secret sits in the middle and knows," Robert Frost wrote, looking in from the outside. Looking out from the inside, Chuang-tzu wrote, "When we understand, we are at the center of the circle, and there we sit while Yes and No chase each other around the circumference." This anonymous center—which is called God in Jewish, Christian, and Moslem cultures, and Tao, Self, or Buddha in the great Eastern traditions—is the realest of realities.

> Self is everywhere, shining forth from all beings,
> vaster than the vast, subtler than the most subtle,
> unreachable, yet nearer than breath, than heartbeat.
> Eye cannot see it, ear cannot hear it nor tongue
> utter it; only in deep absorption can the mind,
> grown pure and silent, merge with the formless truth.
> As soon as you find it, you are free; you have found yourself;
> you have solved the great riddle; your heart forever is at peace.
> Whole, you enter the Whole. Your personal self
> returns to its radiant, intimate, deathless source.
>
> *Mundaka Upanishad*

Most of what we call religious poetry is the poetry of longing: for God, for the mother's face. But the poems in *The Enlightened Heart* are poems of fulfillment. They were written by the Secret, who has many aliases. Sitting or dancing, all these poets have found themselves inside the circle—some of them a step within the circumference, some far in, some at dead center. Looking out from the center, you can talk about the circumference. But really, there is no circumference. Everyone, everything, is joyfully included.

THE
ENLIGHTENED
HEART

The Golden God, the Self, the immortal Swan
leaves the small nest of the body, goes where He wants.
He moves through the realm of dreams; makes numberless
         forms;
delights in sex; eats, drinks, laughs with His friends;
frightens Himself with scenes of heart-chilling terror.
But He is not attached to anything that He sees;
and after He has wandered in the realms of dream and
         awakeness,
has tasted pleasures and experienced good and evil,
He returns to the blissful state from which He began.
As a fish swims forward to one riverbank then the other,
Self alternates between awakeness and dreaming.
As an eagle, weary from long flight, folds its wings,
gliding down to its nest, Self hurries to the realm
of dreamless sleep, free of desires, fear, pain.
As a man in sexual union with his beloved
is unaware of anything outside or inside,
so a man in union with Self knows nothing, wants nothing,
has found his heart's fulfillment and is free of sorrow.
Father disappears, mother disappears, gods
and scriptures disappear, thief disappears, murderer,
rich man, beggar disappear, world disappears,
good and evil disappear; he has passed beyond sorrow.

Two birds, one of them mortal, the other immortal,
live in the same tree. The first one pecks at the fruit,
sweet or bitter; the second looks on without eating.
Thus the personal self pecks at the fruit of this world,
bewildered by suffering, always hungry for more.
But when he meets the True Self, the resplendent God,
the source of creation, all his cravings are stilled.
Perceiving Self in all creatures, he forgets himself
in the service of all; good and evil both vanish;
delighting in Self, playing like a child with Self,
he does whatever is called for, whatever the result.

Self is everywhere, shining forth from all beings,
vaster than the vast, subtler than the most subtle,
unreachable, yet nearer than breath, than heartbeat.
Eye cannot see it, ear cannot hear it nor tongue
utter it; only in deep absorption can the mind,
grown pure and silent, merge with the formless truth.
He who finds it is free; he has found himself;
he has solved the great riddle; his heart forever is at peace.
Whole, he enters the Whole. His personal self
returns to its radiant, intimate, deathless source.
As rivers lose name and form when they disappear
into the sea, the sage leaves behind all traces
when he disappears into the light. Perceiving the truth,
he becomes the truth; he passes beyond all suffering,
beyond death; all the knots of his heart are loosed.

PSALM 1

Blessed are the man and the woman
    who have grown beyond their greed
    and have put an end to their hatred
    and no longer nourish illusions.
But they delight in the way things are
    and keep their hearts open, day and night.
They are like trees planted near flowing rivers,
    which bear fruit when they are ready.
Their leaves will not fall or wither.
    Everything they do will succeed.

PSALM 19

The heavens declare God's glory
     and the magnificence of what made them.
Each new dawn is a miracle;
     each new sky fills with beauty.
Their testimony speaks to the whole world
     and reaches to the ends of the earth.
In them is a path for the sun,
     who steps forth handsome as a bridegroom
     and rejoices like an athlete as he runs.
He starts at one end of the heavens
     and circles to the other end,
     and nothing can hide from his heat.

God's universe is perfect,
     awing the mind.
God's truth is subtle,
     baffling the intellect.
God's law is complete,
     quickening the breath.
God's compassion is fathomless,
     refreshing the soul.
God's justice is absolute,
     lighting up the eyes.
God's love is radiant,
     rejoicing the heart,
more precious than the finest gold,
     sweeter than honey from the comb.

Help me to be aware of my selfishness,
    but without undue shame or self-judgment.
Let me always feel you present,
    in every atom of my life.
Let me keep surrendering my self
    until I am utterly transparent.
Let my words be rooted in honesty
    and my thoughts be lost in your light,
Unnamable God, my essence,
    my origin, my life-blood, my home.

PSALM 104

Unnamable God, you are fathomless;
    I praise you with endless awe.
You are wrapped in light like a cloak;
    you stretch out the sky like a curtain.
You make the clouds your chariot;
    you walk on the wings of the wind.
You use the winds as your messengers,
    thunder and lightning as your servants.
You look at the earth—it trembles;
    you touch the hills and they smoke.
You laid the earth's foundations
    so that they would never be destroyed.
You covered the land with ocean;
    the waters rose higher than the mountains.
They fled at the sound of your voice;
    you thundered and they ran away.
They rushed down into the valleys,
    to the place you appointed for them.
You bounded them, so that they would never
    return to inundate the earth.
You send streams into the valleys,
    and they flow among the hills.
All the animals drink from them;
    the wild asses quench their thirst.
Beside them the birds of the sky dwell,
    singing among the branches.
You water the hills from the sky;

by your care the whole earth is nourished.
You make grass grow for the cattle
    and grains for the service of mankind,
to bring forth food from the earth
    and bread that strengthens the body,
oil that makes the face shine
    and wine that gladdens the heart.
You plant the trees that grow tall,
    pines, and cedars of Lebanon,
in which many birds build their nests,
    and the stork on the topmost branches.
The mountains are for the wild goats;
    the cliffs are a shelter for the rock squirrels.
You created the moon to count months;
    the sun knows when it must set.
You make darkness, it is night,
    the forest animals emerge.
The young lions roar for their prey,
    seeking their food from God.
The sun rises, they withdraw,
    and lie down in their dens.
Man goes out to his labor
    and works until it is evening.
How infinite are your creatures, Unnamable One!
    With wisdom you made them all.
    The whole earth is filled with your riches.
There is the sea in its vastness,
    where innumerable creatures live,
    fish both tiny and huge.
There sharks swim, and the whale
    that you created to play with.

All these depend on you
　　to give them food in due time.
You open your hands—they gather it;
　　you give it—they are filled with gladness.
You hide your face—they are stricken;
　　you take away their breath—they die
　　and return their bodies to the dust.
You send forth your breath—they are born,
　　and with them you replenish the earth.
Your glory will last forever;
　　eternally you rejoice in your works.
I will sing to you at every moment;
　　I will praise you with every breath.
How sweet it is to trust you;
　　what joy to embrace your will.
May all selfishness disappear from me,
　　and may you always shine from my heart.

PSALM 131

Lord, my mind is not noisy with desires,
    and my heart has satisfied its longing.
I do not care about religion
    or anything that is not you.
I have soothed and quieted my soul,
    like a child at its mother's breast.
My soul is as peaceful as a child
    sleeping in its mother's arms.

The tao that can be told
is not the eternal Tao.
The name that can be named
is not the eternal Name.

The unnamable is the eternally real.
Naming is the origin
of all particular things.

Free from desire, you realize the mystery.
Caught in desire, you see only the manifestations.

Yet mystery and manifestations
arise from the same source.
This source is called darkness.

Darkness within darkness.
The gateway to all understanding.

Every being in the universe
is an expression of the Tao.
It springs into existence,
unconscious, perfect, free,
takes on a physical body,
lets circumstances complete it.
That is why every being
spontaneously honors the Tao.

The Tao gives birth to all beings,
nourishes them, maintains them,
cares for them, comforts them, protects them,
takes them back to itself,
creating without possessing,
acting without expecting,
guiding without interfering.
That is why love of the Tao
is in the very nature of things.

The ancient Masters were profound and subtle.
Their wisdom was unfathomable.
There is no way to describe it;
all we can describe is their appearance.

They were careful
as someone crossing an iced-over stream.
Alert as a warrior in enemy territory.
Courteous as a guest.
Fluid as melting ice.
Shapable as a block of wood.
Receptive as a valley.
Clear as a glass of water.

Do you have the patience to wait
till your mud settles and the water is clear?
Can you remain unmoving
till the right action arises by itself?

The Master doesn't seek fulfillment.
Not seeking, not expecting,
she is present, and can welcome all things.

Empty your mind of all thoughts.
Let your heart be at peace.
Watch the turmoil of beings,
but contemplate their return.

Each separate being in the universe
returns to the common source.
Returning to the source is serenity.

If you don't realize the source,
you stumble in confusion and sorrow.
When you realize where you come from,
you naturally become tolerant,
disinterested, amused,
kindhearted as a grandmother,
dignified as a king.
Immersed in the wonder of the Tao,
you can deal with whatever life brings you,
and when death comes, you are ready.

A good traveler has no fixed plans
and is not intent upon arriving.
A good artist lets his intuition
lead him wherever it wants.
A good scientist has freed himself of concepts
and keeps his mind open to what is.

Thus the Master is available to all people
and doesn't reject anyone.
He is ready to use all situations
and doesn't waste anything.
This is called embodying the light.

What is a good man but a bad man's
            teacher?
What is a bad man but a good man's job?
If you don't understand this, you will get lost,
however intelligent you are.
It is the great secret.

Some say that my teaching is nonsense.
Others call it lofty but impractical.
But to those who have looked inside themselves,
this nonsense makes perfect sense.
And to those who put it into practice,
this loftiness has roots that go deep.

I have just three things to teach:
simplicity, patience, compassion.
These three are your greatest treasures.
Simple in actions and in thoughts,
you return to the source of being.
Patient with both friends and enemies,
you accord with the way things are.
Compassionate toward yourself,
you reconcile all beings in the world.

"Those who realize true wisdom,
rapt within this clear awareness,
see me as the universe's
origin, imperishable.

All their words and all their actions
issue from the depths of worship;
held in my embrace, they know me
as a woman knows her lover.

Creatures rise, creatures vanish;
I alone am real, Arjuna,
looking out, amused, from deep
within the eyes of every creature.

I am the object of all knowledge,
father of the world, its mother,
source of all things, of impure and
pure, of holiness and horror.

I am the goal, the root, the witness,
home and refuge, dearest friend,
creation and annihilation,
everlasting seed and treasure.

I am the radiance of the sun, I
open or withhold the rainclouds,
I am immortality and
death, am being and non-being.

I am the Self, Arjuna, seated
in the heart of every creature.
I am the origin, the middle,
and the end that all must come to.

Those who worship me sincerely
with their minds and bodies, giving
up their whole lives in devotion,
find in me their heart's fulfillment.

Even those who do not know me,
if their actions are straightforward,
just, and loving, venerate me
with the truest kind of worship.

All your thoughts, all your actions,
all your fears and disappointments,
offer them to me, clear-hearted;
know them all as passing visions.

Thus you free yourself from bondage,
from both good and evil karma;
through your non-attachment, you
embody me, in utter freedom.

I am justice: clear, impartial,
favoring no one, hating no one.
But in those who have cured themselves of
selfishness, I shine with brilliance.

Even murderers and rapists,
tyrants, the most cruel fanatics,
ultimately know redemption
through my love, if they surrender

to my harsh but healing graces.
Passing through excruciating
transformations, they find freedom
and their hearts find peace within them.

I am always with all beings;
I abandon no one. And
however great your inner darkness,
you are never separate from me.

Let your thoughts flow past you, calmly;
keep me near, at every moment;
trust me with your life, because I
am you, more than you yourself are."

CUTTING UP AN OX

Prince Wen Hui's cook
Was cutting up an ox.
Out went a hand,
Down went a shoulder,
He planted a foot,
He pressed with a knee,
The ox fell apart
With a whisper,
The bright cleaver murmured
Like a gentle wind.
Rhythm! Timing!
Like a sacred dance,
Like "The Mulberry Grove,"
Like ancient harmonies!

"Good work!" the Prince exclaimed,
"Your method is faultless!"
"Method?" said the cook
  Laying aside his cleaver,
"What I follow is Tao
  Beyond all methods!

"When I first began
  To cut up oxen
  I would see before me
  The whole ox
  All in one mass.

"After three years
  I no longer saw this mass.
  I saw the distinctions.

"But now, I see nothing
  With the eye. My whole being
  Apprehends.
  My senses are idle. The spirit
  Free to work without plan
  Follows its own instinct
  Guided by natural line,
  By the secret opening, the hidden space,
  My cleaver finds its own way.
  I cut through no joint, chop no bone.

"A good cook needs a new chopper
  Once a year—he cuts.
  A poor cook needs a new one
  Every month—he hacks!

"I have used this same cleaver
  Nineteen years.
  It has cut up
  A thousand oxen.
  Its edge is as keen
  As if newly sharpened.

"There are spaces in the joints;
  The blade is thin and keen:
  When this thinness
  Finds that space

There is all the room you need!
It goes like a breeze!
Hence I have this cleaver nineteen years
As if newly sharpened!

"True, there are sometimes
  Tough joints. I feel them coming,
  I slow down, I watch closely,
  Hold back, barely move the blade,
  And whump! the part falls away
  Landing like a clod of earth.

"Then I withdraw the blade,
  I stand still
  And let the joy of the work
  Sink in.
  I clean the blade
  And put it away."

  Prince Wen Hui said,
"This is it! My cook has shown me
  How I ought to live
  My own life!"

Translated by Thomas Merton

My heart was split, and a flower
    appeared; and grace sprang up;
    and it bore fruit for my God.
You split me, tore my heart
    open, filled me with love.
You poured your spirit into me;
    I knew you as I know myself.
Speaking waters touched me
    from your fountain, the source of life.
I swallowed them and was drunk
    with the water that never dies.
And my drunkenness was insight,
    intimacy with your spirit.
And you have made all things new;
    you have showed me all things shining.
You have granted me perfect ease;
    I have become like Paradise,
a garden whose fruit is joy;
    and you are the sun upon me.
My eyes are radiant with your spirit;
    my nostrils fill with your fragrance.
My ears delight in your music,
    and my face is covered with your dew.
Blessed are the men and women
    who are planted on your earth, in your garden,
who grow as your trees and flowers grow,
    who transform their darkness to light.
Their roots plunge into darkness;
    their faces turn toward the light.

All those who love you are beautiful;
    they overflow with your presence
    so that they can do nothing but good.
There is infinite space in your garden;
    all men, all women are welcome here;
    all they need do is enter.

THE MIND OF ABSOLUTE TRUST

The Great Way isn't difficult
    for those who are unattached to their preferences.
Let go of longing and aversion,
    and everything will be perfectly clear.
When you cling to a hairbreadth of distinction,
    heaven and earth are set apart.
If you want to realize the truth,
    don't be for or against.
The struggle between good and evil
    is the primal disease of the mind.
Not grasping the deeper meaning,
    you just trouble your mind's serenity.
As vast as infinite space,
    it is perfect and lacks nothing.
But because you select and reject,
    you can't perceive its true nature.
Don't get entangled in the world;
    don't lose yourself in emptiness.
Be at peace in the oneness of things,
    and all errors will disappear by themselves.

If you don't live the Tao,
    you fall into assertion or denial.
Asserting that the world is real,
    you are blind to its deeper reality;
denying that the world is real,
    you are blind to the selflessness of all things.

The more you think about these matters,
    the farther you are from the truth.
Step aside from all thinking,
    and there is nowhere you can't go.
Returning to the root, you find the meaning;
    chasing appearances, you lose their source.
At the moment of profound insight,
    you transcend both appearance and emptiness.
Don't keep searching for the truth;
    just let go of your opinions.

For the mind in harmony with the Tao,
    all selfishness disappears.
With not even a trace of self-doubt,
    you can trust the universe completely.
All at once you are free,
    with nothing left to hold on to.
All is empty, brilliant,
    perfect in its own being.
In the world of things as they are,
    there is no self, no non-self.
If you want to describe its essence,
    the best you can say is "Not-two."
In this "Not-two" nothing is separate,
    and nothing in the world is excluded.
The enlightened of all times and places
    have entered into this truth.
In it there is no gain or loss;
    one instant is ten thousand years.
There is no here, no there;
    infinity is right before your eyes.

The tiny is as large as the vast
        when objective boundaries have vanished;
the vast is as small as the tiny
        when you don't have external limits.
Being is an aspect of non-being;
        non-being is no different from being.
Until you understand this truth,
        you won't see anything clearly.
One is all; all
        are one. When you realize this,
        what reason for holiness or wisdom?
The mind of absolute trust
        is beyond all thought, all striving,
is perfectly at peace, for in it
        there is no yesterday, no today, no tomorrow.

Clambering up the Cold Mountain path,
The Cold Mountain trail goes on and on:
The long gorge choked with scree and boulders,
The wide creek, the mist-blurred grass.
The moss is slippery, though there's been no rain
The pine sings, but there's no wind.
Who can leap the world's ties
And sit with me among the white clouds?

Translated by Gary Snyder

My home was at Cold Mountain from the start,
Rambling among the hills, far from trouble.

Gone, and a million things leave no trace
Loosed, and it flows through the galaxies
A fountain of light, into the very mind—
Not a thing, and yet it appears before me:
Now I know the pearl of the Buddha-nature
Know its use: a boundless perfect sphere.

Translated by Gary Snyder

You ask why I make my home in the mountain forest,
and I smile, and am silent,
and even my soul remains quiet:
it lives in the other world
which no one owns.
The peach trees blossom.
The water flows.

Translated by Sam Hamill

The birds have vanished into the sky,
and now the last cloud drains away.

We sit together, the mountain and me,
until only the mountain remains.

Translated by Sam Hamill

WRITTEN ON THE WALL AT
CHANG'S HERMITAGE

It is Spring in the mountains.
I come alone seeking you.
The sound of chopping wood echoes
Between the silent peaks.
The streams are still icy.
There is snow on the trail.
At sunset I reach your grove
In the stony mountain pass.
You want nothing, although at night
You can see the aura of gold
And silver ore all around you.
You have learned to be gentle
As the mountain deer you have tamed.
The way back forgotten, hidden
Away, I become like you,
An empty boat, floating, adrift.

Translated by Kenneth Rexroth

When the mind is at peace,
the world too is at peace.
Nothing real, nothing absent.
Not holding on to reality,
not getting stuck in the void,
you are neither holy nor wise, just
an ordinary fellow who has completed his work.

My daily affairs are quite ordinary;
but I'm in total harmony with them.
I don't hold on to anything, don't reject anything;
nowhere an obstacle or conflict.
Who cares about wealth and honor?
Even the poorest thing shines.
My miraculous power and spiritual activity:
drawing water and carrying wood.

SINGING IMAGE OF FIRE

A hand moves, and the fire's whirling takes different shapes:
All things change when we do.
The first word, "Ah," blossoms into all others.
Each of them is true.

Translated by Jane Hirshfield

If you look for the truth outside yourself,
it gets farther and farther away.
Today, walking alone,
I meet him everywhere I step.
He is the same as me,
yet I am not him.
Only if you understand it in this way
will you merge with the way things are.

We awaken in Christ's body
as Christ awakens our bodies,
and my poor hand is Christ, He enters
my foot, and is infinitely me.

I move my hand, and wonderfully
my hand becomes Christ, becomes all of Him
(for God is indivisibly
whole, seamless in His Godhood).

I move my foot, and at once
He appears like a flash of lightning.
Do my words seem blasphemous?—Then
open your heart to Him

and let yourself receive the one
who is opening to you so deeply.
For if we genuinely love Him,
we wake up inside Christ's body

where all our body, all over,
every most hidden part of it,
is realized in joy as Him,
and He makes us, utterly, real,

and everything that is hurt, everything
that seemed to us dark, harsh, shameful,
maimed, ugly, irreparably
damaged, is in Him transformed

and recognized as whole, as lovely,
and radiant in His light
we awaken as the Beloved
in every last part of our body.

Watching the moon
at dawn,
solitary, mid-sky,
I knew myself completely:
no part left out.

Translated by Jane Hirshfield with Mariko Aratani

The roaring waterfall
is the Buddha's golden mouth.
The mountains in the distance
are his pure luminous body.
How many thousands of poems
have flowed through me tonight!
And tomorrow I won't be able
to repeat even one word.

Holy Spirit,
giving life to all life,
moving all creatures,
root of all things,
washing them clean,
wiping out their mistakes,
healing their wounds,
you are our true life,
luminous, wonderful,
awakening the heart
from its ancient sleep.

CANTICLE OF THE SUN

Most high, all-powerful sweet Lord,
yours is the praise, the glory, and the honor
and every blessing.

Be praised, my Lord,
for all your creatures,
and first for brother sun,
who makes the day bright and luminous.

And he is beautiful and radiant
    with great splendor,
he is the image of you, Most High.

Be praised, my Lord,
for sister moon and the stars,
in the sky you have made them brilliant and precious and
        beautiful.

Be praised, my Lord, for brother wind
and for the air both cloudy and serene
    and every kind of weather,
through which you give nourishment
    to your creatures.

Be praised, my Lord, for sister water,
who is very useful and humble
    and precious and chaste.

43

Be praised, my Lord, for brother fire,
through whom you illuminate the night.
And he is beautiful and joyous
    and robust and strong.

Be praised, my Lord,
    for our sister, mother earth,
who nourishes us and watches over us
and brings forth various fruits
    with colored flowers and herbs.

Be praised, my Lord,
    for those who forgive through your love,
and bear sickness and tribulation;

blessed are those who endure in peace,
for they will be crowned by you, Most High.

Be praised, my Lord,
    for our sister, bodily death,
from whom no living thing can escape.

Blessed are those whom she finds
    doing your most holy will,
for the second death cannot harm them.

Praise and bless my Lord
and give thanks to him and serve him
    with great humility.

One instant is eternity;
eternity is the now.
When you see through this one instant,
you see through the one who sees.

The Great Way has no gate;
there are a thousand paths to it.
If you pass through the barrier,
you walk the universe alone.

Ten thousand flowers in spring, the moon in autumn,
a cool breeze in summer, snow in winter.
If your mind isn't clouded by unnecessary things,
this is the best season of your life.

Moon and clouds are the same;
mountain and valley are different.
All are blessed; all are blessed.
Is this one? Is this two?

ON THE TREASURY
OF THE TRUE DHARMA EYE

Midnight. No waves,
no wind, the empty boat
is flooded with moonlight.

ON NON-DEPENDENCE OF MIND

Coming, going, the waterbirds
don't leave a trace,
don't follow a path.

Don't grieve. Anything you lose comes round
in another form. The child weaned from mother's milk
now drinks wine and honey mixed.

God's joy moves from unmarked box to unmarked box,
from cell to cell. As rainwater, down into flowerbed.
As roses, up from ground.
Now it looks like a plate of rice and fish,
now a cliff covered with vines,
now a horse being saddled.
It hides within these,
till one day it cracks them open.

Part of the self leaves the body when we sleep
and changes shape. You might say, "Last night
I was a cypress tree, a small bed of tulips,
a field of grapevines." Then the phantasm goes away.
You're back in the room.
I don't want to make anyone fearful.
Hear what's behind what I say.

Ta dum dum, taaa dum, ta ta dum.
There's the light gold of wheat in the sun
and the gold of bread made from that wheat.
I have neither. I'm only talking about them,

as a town in the desert looks up
at stars on a clear night.

Translated by Coleman Barks with A. J. Arberry

Morning: a polished knifeblade,
the smell of white camphor burning.

The sky tears his blue Sufi robe
deliberately in half.

Daylight Rumi drags his dark opposite
out of sight. A happy Turk comes in.
A grieving Hindu leaves.

The King of the Ethiopians goes.
Caesar arrives.

No one knows how what changes,
changes.

One half of the planet is grass.
The other half grazing.

A pearl goes up for auction. No one has enough,
so the pearl buys itself.

We stand beside Noah and David and Rabia
and Jesus and Muhammed.

Quietness again lifts and planes out,
the blood in our heads gliding
in the sky of the brain.

Translated by Coleman Barks with A. J. Arberry

When grapes turn
to wine, they long for our ability to change.

When stars wheel
around the North Pole,
they are longing for our growing consciousness.

Wine got drunk with us,
not the other way.
The body developed out of us, not we from it.

We are bees,
and our body is a honeycomb.
We made
the body, cell by cell we made it.

Translated by Robert Bly

Totally conscious, and apropos of nothing, he comes to see me.
Is someone here? I ask.
The moon. The full moon is inside your house.

My friends and I go running out into the street.
I'm in here, comes a voice from the house, but we aren't
        listening.
We're looking up at the sky.
My pet nightingale sobs like a drunk in the garden.
Ringdoves scatter with small cries, *Where, Where.*
It's midnight. The whole neighborhood is up and out in
        the street
thinking, *The cat-burglar has come back.*
The actual thief is there too, saying out loud,
Yes, the cat-burglar is somewhere in this crowd.
No one pays attention.

Lo, I am with you always, means when you look for God,
God is in the look of your eyes,
in the thought of looking, nearer to you than your self,
or things that have happened to you.
There's no need to go outside.
Be melting snow.
Wash yourself of yourself.

A white flower grows in the quietness.
Let your tongue become that flower.

Translated by Coleman Barks with A. J. Arberry

I have lived on the lip
of insanity, wanting to know reasons,
knocking on a door. It opens.
I've been knocking from the inside!

Translated by Coleman Barks with John Moyne

Forget your life. Say *God is Great.* Get up.
You think you know what time it is. It's time to pray.
You've carved so many little figurines, too many.
Don't knock on any random door like a beggar.
Reach your long hand out to another door, beyond where
you go on the street, the street
where everyone says, "How are you?"
and no one says *How aren't you?*

Tomorrow you'll see what you've broken and torn tonight,
thrashing in the dark. Inside you
there's an artist you don't know about.
He's not interested in how things look different in moonlight.

If you are here unfaithfully with us,
you're causing terrible damage.
If you've opened your loving to God's love,
you're helping people you don't know
and have never seen.

Is what I say true? Say *yes* quickly,
if you know, if you've known it
from before the beginning of the universe.

Translated by Coleman Barks with A. J. Arberry

All day and night, music,
a quiet, bright
reedsong. If it
fades, we fade.

Translated by Coleman Barks with John Moyne

You are the notes, and we are the flute.
We are the mountain, you are the sounds coming down.
We are the pawns and kings and rooks
you set out on a board: we win or we lose.
We are lions rolling and unrolling on flags.
Your invisible wind carries us through the world.

Translated by Robert Bly

Out beyond ideas of wrongdoing and rightdoing,
there is a field. I'll meet you there.

When the soul lies down in that grass,
the world is too full to talk about.
Ideas, language, even the phrase *each other*
doesn't make any sense.

Translated by Coleman Barks with John Moyne

The drunkards are rolling in slowly, those who hold to wine are
        approaching.
The lovers come, singing, from the garden, the ones with
        brilliant eyes.

The I-don't-want-to-lives are leaving, and the I-want-to-lives
        are arriving.
They have gold sewn into their clothes, sewn in for those who
        have none.

Those with ribs showing who have been grazing in the old
        pasture of love
are turning up fat and frisky.

The souls of pure teachers are arriving like rays of sunlight
from so far up to the ground-huggers.

How marvellous is that garden, where apples and pears, both for
        the sake of the two Marys,
are arriving even in winter.

Those apples grow from the Gift, and sink back into the Gift.
It must be that they are coming from the garden to the garden.

Translated by Robert Bly

Outside, the freezing desert night.
This other night inside grows warm, kindling.
Let the landscape be covered with thorny crust.
We have a soft garden in here.
The continents blasted,
cities and little towns, everything
become a scorched, blackened ball.

The news we hear is full of grief for that future,
but the real news inside here
is there's no news at all.

Translated by Coleman Barks with John Moyne

When it's cold and raining,
You are more beautiful.

And the snow brings me
even closer to Your Lips.

The Inner Secret, that which was never born,
You are That Freshness, and I am with You now.

I can't explain the goings,
or the comings. You enter suddenly,

and I am nowhere again.
Inside the Majesty.

Translated by Coleman Barks with A. J. Arberry

Praise to the emptiness that blanks out existence. Existence:
This place made from our love for that emptiness!
Yet somehow comes emptiness,
this existence goes.
Praise to that happening, over and over!

For years I pulled my own existence out of emptiness.
Then one swoop, one swing of the arm,
that work is over.
Free of who I was, free of presence, free of
dangerous fear, hope,
free of mountainous wanting.
The here-and-now mountain is a tiny piece of a piece
of straw
blown off into emptiness.

These words I'm saying so much begin to lose meaning:
Existence, emptiness, mountain, straw:
Words and what they try to say swept
out the window, down the slant of the roof.

Translated by Coleman Barks with John Moyne

A fish cannot drown in water,
A bird does not fall in air.
In the fire of creation,
Gold doesn't vanish:
The fire brightens.
Each creature God made
Must live in its own true nature;
How could I resist my nature,
That lives for oneness with God?

Translated by Jane Hirshfield

Effortlessly,
Love flows from God into man,
Like a bird
Who rivers the air
Without moving her wings.
Thus we move in His world
One in body and soul,
Though outwardly separate in form.
As the Source strikes the note,
Humanity sings—
The Holy Spirit is our harpist,
And all strings
Which are touched in Love
Must sound.

Translated by Jane Hirshfield

Of all that God has shown me
I can speak just the smallest word,
Not more than a honey bee
Takes on her foot
From an overspilling jar.

Translated by Jane Hirshfield

"This mountain of release is such that the
          ascent's most painful at the start, below;
          the more you rise, the milder it will be.
     And when the slope feels gentle to the point that
          climbing up sheer rock is effortless
          as though you were gliding downstream in a boat,
     then you will have arrived where this path ends."

"The love of God, unutterable and perfect,
    flows into a pure soul the way that light
    rushes into a transparent object.
The more love that it finds, the more it gives
    itself; so that, as we grow clear and open,
    the more complete the joy of heaven is.
And the more souls who resonate together,
    the greater the intensity of their love,
    and, mirror-like, each soul reflects the other."

"But you who are so happy here, tell me:
     do you aspire to a more profound
     insight, or a greater ecstasy?"
She smiled a little, as did the shades beside her;
     then answered with such gladness that her whole
     being seemed to glow with love's first fire:
"Brother, God's generosity itself
     calms our will, and makes us want no more
     than what we have, and long for nothing else.
If we desired any greater bliss,
     we would not be in harmony with Him
     whose love assigns us to a lower place.
The essence of this joy is that we all
     have given up our personal desires
     so that our will is merged with God's own will.
Therefore our rank in heaven, from height to height,
     is just as dear to each particular soul
     as to the Master who appointed it.
In His will is our peace: it is the sea
     into which all currents and all streams
     empty themselves, for all eternity."

Between the conscious and the unconscious, the mind has put
       up a swing:
all earth creatures, even the supernovas, sway between these
       two trees,
and it never winds down.

Angels, animals, humans, insects by the million, also the
       wheeling sun and moon;
ages go by, and it goes on.

Everything is swinging: heaven, earth, water, fire,
and the secret one slowly growing a body.
Kabir saw that for fifteen seconds, and it made him a servant
       for life.

Translated by Robert Bly

Inside this clay jar there are meadows and groves and the One
who made them.

Inside this jar there are seven oceans and innumerable stars, acid
to test gold, and a patient appraiser of jewels.

Inside this jar the music of eternity, and a spring flows from the
source of all waters.

Kabir says: Listen, friend! My beloved Master lives inside.

Translated by Czeslaw Milosz and Robert Hass

Are you looking for me? I am in the next seat.
My shoulder is against yours.
You will not find me in stupas, not in Indian shrine rooms, nor in
        synagogues, nor in cathedrals:
not in masses, nor kirtans, not in legs winding around your own
        neck, nor in eating nothing but vegetables.
When you really look for me, you will see me instantly—
you will find me in the tiniest house of time.
Kabir says: Student, tell me, what is God?
He is the breath inside the breath.

My friend, this body is His lute. He tightens the strings and plays
     its songs.

If the strings break and the pegs work loose, this lute, made of
     dust, returns to dust.

Kabir says: Nobody else can wake from it that heavenly music.

Translated by Czeslaw Milosz and Robert Hass

I have been thinking of the difference between water
and the waves on it. Rising,
water's still water, falling back,
it is water, will you give me a hint
how to tell them apart?

Because someone has made up the word
"wave," do I have to distinguish it
from water?

There is a Secret One inside us;
the planets in all the galaxies
pass through his hands like beads.

That is a string of beads one should look at with luminous eyes.

Translated by Robert Bly

Swan, tell me your old story.

What country have you come from, swan, what shores are you
flying to?

Where do you rest at night, and what are you looking for?

It's dawn, swan, wake up, soar to the air, follow me!

There is a land not governed by sadness and doubt, where the
fear of death is unknown.

Spring forests bloom there and the wind is sweet with the flower
He-Is-Myself.

The bee of the heart dives into it and wants no other joy.

Translated by Czeslaw Milosz and Robert Hass

Student, do the simple purification.
You know that the seed is inside the horse-chestnut tree;
and inside the seed there are the blossoms of the tree, and the
          chestnuts, and the shade.
So inside the human body there is the seed, and inside the seed
          there is the human body again.

Fire, air, earth, water, and space—if you don't want the secret
          one,
you can't have these either.

Thinkers, listen, tell me what you know of that is not inside
          the soul?
Take a pitcher full of water and set it down on the water—
now it has water inside and water outside.
We mustn't give it a name,
lest silly people start talking again about the body and the soul.

If you want the truth, I'll tell you the truth:
Listen to the secret sound, the real sound, which is inside you.
The one no one talks of speaks the secret sound to himself,
and he is the one who has made it all.

Translated by Robert Bly

WHY MIRA CAN'T GO BACK
TO HER OLD HOUSE

The colors of the Dark One have penetrated Mira's body; all the
    other colors washed out.

Making love with the Dark One and eating little, those are my
    pearls and my carnelians.

Meditation beads and the forehead streak, those are my scarves
    and my rings.

That's enough feminine wiles for me. My teacher taught me this.

Approve me or disapprove me: I praise the Mountain Energy
    night and day.

I take the path that ecstatic human beings have taken for
    centuries.

I don't steal money, I don't hit anyone. What will you charge me
    with?

I have felt the swaying of the elephant's shoulders; and now you
    want me to climb on a jackass? Try to be serious.

Translated by Robert Bly

THE CLOUDS

When I saw the dark clouds, I wept, Oh Dark One, I wept at the
dark clouds.

Black clouds soared up, and took some yellow along; rain did
fall, some rain fell long.

There was water east of the house, west of the house; fields all
green.

The one I love lives past those fields; rain has fallen on my body,
on my hair, as I wait in the open door for him.

The Energy that holds up mountains is the energy Mirabai bows
down to.

He lives century after century, and the test I set for him he has
passed.

Translated by Robert Bly

O my friends,
What can you tell me of Love,
Whose pathways are filled with strangeness?
When you offer the Great One your love,
At the first step your body is crushed.
Next be ready to offer your head as his seat.
Be ready to orbit his lamp like a moth giving in to the light,
To live in the deer as she runs toward the hunter's call,
In the partridge that swallows hot coals for love of the moon,
In the fish that, kept from the sea, happily dies.
Like a bee trapped for life in the closing of the sweet flower,
Mira has offered herself to her Lord.
She says, the single Lotus will swallow you whole.

Translated by Jane Hirshfield

"Be cheerful, sir:
Our revels now are ended. These our actors,
As I foretold you, were all spirits and
Are melted into air, into thin air:
And, like the baseless fabric of this vision,
The cloud-capp'd towers, the gorgeous palaces,
The solemn temples, the great globe itself,
Yea, all which it inherit, shall dissolve
And, like this insubstantial pageant faded,
Leave not a rack behind. We are such stuff
As dreams are made on, and our little life
Is rounded with a sleep."

PRAYER

Prayer, the Church's banquet, Angels' age,
    God's breath in man returning to his birth,
    The soul in paraphrase, heart in pilgrimage,
The Christian plummet sounding heaven and earth;
Engine against the Almighty, sinner's tower,
    Reversèd thunder, Christ-side-piercing spear,
    The six-days' world transposing in an hour,
A kind of tune, which all things hear and fear;
Softness, and peace, and joy, and love, and bliss,
    Exalted Manna, gladness of the best,
    Heaven in ordinary, man well drest,
The milky way, the bird of Paradise,
    Church-bells beyond the stars heard, the soul's blood,
    The land of spices; something understood.

THE ELIXIR

Teach me, my God and King,
In all things thee to see,
And what I do in any thing,
To do it as for thee:

Not rudely, as a beast,
To run into an action;
But still to make thee prepossessed,
And give it his perfection.

A man that looks on glass,
On it may stay his eye;
Or if he pleaseth, through it pass,
And then the heaven espy.

All may of thee partake:
Nothing can be so mean,
Which with his tincture (for thy sake)
Will not grow bright and clean.

A servant with this clause
Makes drudgery divine:
Who sweeps a room, as for thy laws,
Makes that and the action fine.

This is the famous stone
That turneth all to gold:
For that which God doth touch and own
Cannot for less be told.

LOVE

Love bade me welcome; yet my soul drew back,
      Guilty of dust and sin.
But quick-eyed Love, observing me grow slack
      From my first entrance in,
Drew nearer to me, sweetly questioning,
      If I lacked any thing.

"A guest," I answered, "worthy to be here":
      Love said, "You shall be he."
"I the unkind, ungrateful? Ah my dear,
      I cannot look on thee."
Love took my hand, and smiling did reply,
      "Who made the eyes but I?"

"Truth, Lord, but I have marred them: let my shame
      Go where it doth deserve."
"And know you not," says Love, "who bore the blame?"
      "My dear, then I will serve."
"You must sit down," says Love, "and taste my meat":
      So I did sit and eat.

Die while you're alive
and be absolutely dead.
Then do whatever you want:
it's all good.

POEM WITHOUT A CATEGORY

Trailing my stick I go down to the garden edge,
call to a monk to go out the pine gate.
A cup of tea with my mother,
looking at each other, enjoying our tea together.
In the deep lanes, few people in sight;
the dog barks when anyone comes or goes.
Fall floods have washed away the planks of the bridge;
shouldering our sandals, we wade the narrow stream.
By the roadside, a small pavilion
where there used to be a little hill:
it helps out our hermit mood;
country poems pile one sheet on another.
I dabble in the flow, delighted by the shallowness of the stream,
gaze at the flagging, admiring how firm the stones are.
The point in life is to know what's enough—
why envy those otherworld immortals?
With the happiness held in one inch-square heart
you can fill the whole space between heaven and earth.

Translated by Burton Watson

God, whose love and joy
          are present everywhere,
can't come to visit you
          unless you aren't there.

IT DEPENDS ON YOU

If in your heart you make
    a manger for his birth,
then God will once again
    become a child on earth.

God is a pure no-thing,
        concealed in now and here:
the less you reach for him,
        the more he will appear.

THE SALUTATION

These little limbs,
These eyes and hands which here I find,
These rosy cheeks wherewith my life begins,
Where have ye been? Behind
What curtain were ye from me hid so long!
Where was, in what abyss, my speaking tongue?

When silent I
So many thousand thousand years
Beneath the dust did in a chaos lie,
How could I smiles or tears,
Or lips or hands or eyes or ears perceive?
Welcome, ye treasures, which I now receive.

I that so long
Was nothing from eternity,
Did little think such joys as ear or tongue
To celebrate or see:
Such sounds to hear, such hands to feel, such feet,
Beneath the skies, on such a ground to meet.

New burnished joys!
Which yellow gold and pearl excel!
Such sacred treasures are the limbs of boys,
In which a soul doth dwell;
Their organizèd joints and azure veins
More wealth include than all the world contains.

From dust I rise,
And out of nothing now awake;
These brighter regions which salute mine eyes
A gift from God I take.
The earth, the seas, the light, the day, the skies,
The sun and stars are mine; if those I prize.

Long time before
I in my mother's womb was born,
A God preparing did this glorious store,
The world for me adorn.
Into this Eden so divine and fair,
So wide and bright, I come, his son and heir.

A stranger here
Strange things doth meet, strange glories see;
Strange treasures lodged in this fair world appear,
Strange all, and new to me.
But that they mine should be, who nothing was,
That strangest is of all, yet brought to pass.

Old pond,
frog jumps in—
splash.

Translated by Michael Katz

Though I'm in Kyoto,
when the cuckoo sings
I long for Kyoto.

Translated by John Tarrant

To see a World in a Grain of Sand
And a Heaven in a Wild Flower,
Hold Infinity in the palm of your hand
And Eternity in an hour.

ETERNITY

He who binds to himself a joy
Does the winged life destroy.
But he who kisses the joy as it flies
Lives in eternity's sun rise.

First days of spring—the sky
is bright blue, the sun huge and warm.
Everything's turning green.
Carrying my monk's bowl, I walk to the village
to beg for my daily meal.
The children spot me at the temple gate
and happily crowd around,
dragging at my arms till I stop.
I put my bowl on a white rock,
hang my bag on a branch.
First we braid grasses and play tug-of-war,
then we take turns singing and keeping a kick-ball in the air:
I kick the ball and they sing, they kick and I sing.
Time is forgotten, the hours fly.
People passing by point at me and laugh:
"Why are you acting like such a fool?"
I nod my head and don't answer.
I could say something, but why?
Do you want to know what's in my heart?
From the beginning of time: just this! just this!

In all ten directions of the universe,
there is only one truth.
When we see clearly, the great teachings are the same.
What can ever be lost? What can be attained?
If we attain something, it was there from the beginning of time.
If we lose something, it is hiding somewhere near us.
Look: this ball in my pocket:
can you see how priceless it is?

Too lazy to be ambitious,
I let the world take care of itself.
Ten days' worth of rice in my bag;
a bundle of twigs by the fireplace.
Why chatter about delusion and enlightenment?
Listening to the night rain on my roof,
I sit comfortably, with both legs stretched out.

The man pulling radishes
pointed the way
with a radish.

Translated by Robert Hass

In the cherry blossom's shade
there's no such thing
as a stranger.

Flying out from
the Great Buddha's nose:
a swallow.

For the raindrop, joy is in entering the river—
Unbearable pain becomes its own cure.

Travel far enough into sorrow, tears turn to sighing;
In this way we learn how water can die into air.

When, after heavy rain, the stormclouds disperse,
Is it not that they've wept themselves clear to the end?

If you want to know the miracle, how wind can polish a mirror,
Look: the shining glass grows green in spring.

It's the rose's unfolding, Ghalib, that creates the desire to see—
In every color and circumstance, may the eyes be open for what
    comes.

Translated by Jane Hirshfield

The world is no more than the Beloved's single face;
In the desire of the One to know its own beauty, we exist.

Each place, each moment, sings its particular song of not-being
          and being.
Without reason, the clear glass equally mirrors wisdom and
          madness.

Those who claim knowledge are wrong; prayer just leads to
          trance;
Appearance and faith are mere lees in the Unknowing Wine.

Wherever the Footprint is found,
that handful of dust holds the oneness of worlds.

This earth, burnished by hearing the Name, is so certain of Love
That the sky bends unceasingly down, to greet its own light.

Translated by Jane Hirshfield

The colors of tulips and roses are not the same,
Yet in each we assent to the single Spring.

We turn our hands to the sketchbook only for Love:
Needing some pretext for meeting.

What sorry man drinks for pleasure?
Night and day, I raise oblivion's glass.

In the hour of forgetfulness, the head lies by the wine-jar;
In the hour of prayer, the face turns to the Call.

Let me be clear: however the world's goblet turns,
Those who know are always drunk on the wine of the Self.

Translated by Jane Hirshfield

Even at prayer, our eyes look inward;
If the gate to the holy is shut, we just turn away.

The One is only the One, everyone knows—
What mirroring icon could hold it face to face?

Held back unvoiced, grief bruises the heart;
Not reaching the river, a raindrop is swallowed by dust.

If a story brings only tears and not blood to the eyes,
It is simply a lovers' tale.

Whoever can't see the whole in every part plays at blind
            man's buff;
A wise man tastes the entire Tigris in every sip.

Translated by Jane Hirshfield

Let the ascetics sing of the garden of Paradise—
We who dwell in the true ecstasy can forget their vase-tamed
        bouquet.

In our hall of mirrors, the map of the one Face appears
As the sun's splendor would spangle a world made of dew.

Hidden in this image is also its end,
As peasants' lives harbor revolt and unthreshed corn sparks
        with fire.

Hidden in my silence are a thousand abandoned longings:
My words the darkened oil lamp on a stranger's unspeaking
        grave.

Ghalib, the road of change is before you always:
The only line stitching this world's scattered parts.

Translated by Jane Hirshfield

Before there was a trace of this world of men,
I carried the memory of a lock of your hair,
A stray end gathered within me, though unknown.

Inside that invisible realm,
Your face like the sun longed to be seen,
Until each separate object was finally flung into vision.

From the moment of time's first-drawn breath,
Love resides in us,
A treasure locked into the heart's hidden vault.

Before the first seed broke open the rosebed of Being,
An inner lark soared through your meadows,
Heading towards Home.

What can I do but thank you, one hundred times?
Your face illumines the shrine of Hayati's eyes,
Constantly present and lovely.

Translated by Jane Hirshfield

Trippers and askers surround me,
People I meet. . . . the effect upon me of my early life. . . . of the
        ward and city I live in. . . . of the nation,
The latest news. . . . discoveries, inventions, societies. . . .
        authors old and new,
My dinner, dress, associates, looks, business, compliments, dues,
The real or fancied indifference of some man or woman I love,
The sickness of one of my folks—or of myself. . . . or ill-
        doing. . . . or loss or lack of money. . . . or depressions
        or exaltations,
These come to me days and nights and go from me again,
But they are not the Me myself.

Apart from the pulling and hauling stands what I am,
Stands amused, complacent, compassionating, idle, unitary,
Looks down, is erect, bends an arm on an impalpable certain
        rest,
Looks with its sidecurved head, curious what will come next,
Both in and out of the game, and watching and wondering at it.

Backward I see in my own days where I sweated through fog
        with linguists and contenders,
I have no mockings or arguments. . . . I witness and wait.

I believe in you my soul. . . . the other I am must not abase itself
        to you,
And you must not be abased to the other.

Loafe with me on the grass. . . . loose the stop from your throat,
Not words, not music or rhyme I want. . . . not custom or
        lecture, not even the best,
Only the lull I like, the hum of your valved voice.

I mind how we lay in June, such a transparent summer morning;
You settled your head athwart my hips and gently turned over
        upon me,
And parted the shirt from my bosom-bone, and plunged your
        tongue to my barestript heart,
And reached till you felt my beard, and reached till you held
        my feet.
Swiftly arose and spread around me the peace and knowledge
        that pass all the arguments of the earth;
And I know that the hand of God is the elderhand of my own,
And I know that the spirit of God is the eldest brother of my
        own,
And that all the men ever born are also my brothers. . . . and the
        women my sisters and lovers,
And that a kelson of the creation is love;
And limitless are leaves stiff or drooping in the fields,
And brown ants in the little wells beneath them,
And mossy scabs of the wormfence, and heaped stones, and
        elder and mullen and pokeweed.

I have said that the soul is not more than the body,
And I have said that the body is not more than the soul,
And nothing, not God, is greater to one than one's-self is,
And whoever walks a furlong without sympathy walks to his
          own funeral, dressed in his shroud,
And I or you pocketless of a dime may purchase the pick of
          the earth,
And to glance with an eye or show a bean in its pod confounds
          the learning of all times,
And there is no trade or employment but the young man
          following it may become a hero,
And there is no object so soft but it makes a hub for the wheeled
          universe,
And any man or woman shall stand cool and supercilious before
          a million universes.

And I call to mankind, Be not curious about God,
For I who am curious about each am not curious about God,
No array of terms can say how much I am at peace about God
          and about death.

I hear and behold God in every object, yet I understand God not
          in the least,
Nor do I understand who there can be more wonderful than
          myself.

Why should I wish to see God better than this day?
I see something of God in each hour of the twenty-four, and each
          moment then,

In the faces of men and women I see God, and in my own face in
        the glass;
I find letters from God dropped in the street, and every one is
        signed by God's name,
And I leave them where they are, for I know that others will
        punctually come forever and ever.

And as to you death, and you bitter hug of mortality. . . . it is
        idle to try to alarm me.

To his work without flinching the accoucheur comes,
I see the elderhand pressing receiving supporting,
I recline by the sills of the exquisite flexible doors. . . . and mark
        the outlet, and mark the relief and escape.

And as to you corpse, I think you are good manure, but that
        does not offend me,
I smell the white roses sweetscented and growing,
I reach to the leafy lips. . . . I reach to the polished breasts of
        melons.

And as to you life, I reckon you are the leavings of many deaths,
No doubt I have died myself ten thousand times before.

I hear you whispering there O stars of heaven,
O suns. . . . O grass of graves. . . . O perpetual transfers and
        promotions. . . . if you do not say anything how can I
        say anything?

Of the turbid pool that lies in the autumn forest,
Of the moon that descends the steeps of the soughing twilight,

Toss, sparkles of day and dusk. . . . toss on the black stems that
    decay in the muck,
Toss to the moaning gibberish of the dry limbs.

I ascend from the moon. . . . I ascend from the night,
And perceive of the ghastly glimmer the sunbeams reflected,
And debouch to the steady and central from the offspring great
    or small.

There is that in me. . . . I do not know what it is. . . . but I know
    it is in me.

Wrenched and sweaty. . . . calm and cool then my body
    becomes;
I sleep. . . . I sleep long.

I do not know it. . . . it is without name. . . . it is a word unsaid,
It is not in any dictionary or utterance or symbol.

Something it swings on more than the earth I swing on,
To it the creation is the friend whose embracing awakes me.

Perhaps I might tell more. . . . Outlines! I plead for my brothers
    and sisters.

Do you see O my brothers and sisters?
It is not chaos or death. . . . It is form and union and plan. . . . it
    is eternal life. . . . it is happiness.

I dwell in Possibility—
A fairer House than Prose—
More numerous of Windows—
Superior—for Doors—

Of Chambers as the Cedars—
Impregnable of Eye—
And for an Everlasting Roof
The Gambrels of the Sky—

Of Visitors—the fairest—
For Occupation—This—
The spreading wide my narrow Hands
To gather Paradise—

Not "Revelation"—'tis—that waits,
But our unfurnished eyes—

The Soul's Superior instants
Occur to Her—alone—
When friend—and Earth's occasion
Have infinite withdrawn—

Or She—Herself—ascended
To too remote a Height
For lower Recognition
Than Her Omnipotent—

This Mortal Abolition
Is seldom—but as fair
As Apparition—subject
To Autocratic Air—

Eternity's disclosure
To favorites—a few—
Of the Colossal substance
Of Immortality

The Brain—is wider than the Sky—
For—put them side by side—
The one the other will contain
With ease—and You—beside—

The Brain is deeper than the sea—
For—hold them—Blue to Blue—
The one the other will absorb—
As Sponges—Buckets—do—

The Brain is just the weight of God—
For—Heft them—Pound for Pound—
And they will differ—if they do—
As Syllable from Sound—

Nature—the Gentlest Mother is,
Impatient of no Child—
The feeblest—or the waywardest—
Her Admonition mild—

In Forest—and the Hill—
By Traveller—be heard—
Restraining Rampant Squirrel—
Or too impetuous Bird—

How fair Her Conversation—
A Summer Afternoon—
Her Household—Her Assembly—
And when the Sun go down—

Her Voice among the Aisles
Incite the timid prayer
Of the minutest Cricket—
The most unworthy Flower—

When all the Children sleep—
She turns as long away
As will suffice to light Her lamps—
Then bending from the Sky—

With infinite Affection—
And infiniter Care—
Her Golden finger on Her lip—
Wills Silence—Everywhere—

As kingfishers catch fire, dragonflies draw flame;
As tumbled over rim in roundy wells
Stones ring; like each tucked string tells, each hung bell's
Bow swung finds tongue to fling out broad its name;
Each mortal thing does one thing and the same:
Deals out that being indoors each one dwells;
Selves—goes its self; *myself* it speaks and spells,
Crying *What I do is me: for that I came.*

I say more: the just man justices;
Keeps grace: that keeps all his goings graces;
Acts in God's eye what in God's eye he is—
Christ—for Christ plays in ten thousand places,
Lovely in limbs, and lovely in eyes not his
To the Father through the features of men's faces.

GOD'S GRANDEUR

The world is charged with the grandeur of God.
    It will flame out, like shining from shook foil;
    It gathers to a greatness, like the ooze of oil
Crushed. Why do men then now not reck his rod?
Generations have trod, have trod, have trod;
    And all is seared with trade; bleared, smeared with toil;
    And wears man's smudge and shares man's smell: the soil
Is bare now, nor can foot feel, being shod.

And for all this, nature is never spent;
    There lives the dearest freshness deep down things;
And though the last lights off the black West went
    Oh, morning, at the brown brink eastward, springs—
Because the Holy Ghost over the bent
    World broods with warm breast and with ah! bright wings.

PIED BEAUTY

Glory be to God for dappled things—
    For skies of couple-colour as a brinded cow;
        For rose-moles all in stipple upon trout that swim;
Fresh-firecoal chestnut-falls; finches' wings;
    Landscape plotted and pieced—fold, fallow, and plough;
        And all trades, their gear and tackle and trim.

All things counter, original, spare, strange;
    Whatever is fickle, freckled (who knows how?)
        With swift, slow; sweet, sour; adazzle, dim;
He fathers-forth whose beauty is past change:
            Praise him.

THAT NATURE IS A HERACLITEAN FIRE
AND OF THE
COMFORT OF THE RESURRECTION

Cloud-puffball, torn tufts, tossed pillows ' flaunt forth, then
      chevy on an air-
built thoroughfare: heaven-roysterers, in gay-gangs ' they
      throng; they glitter in marches.
Down roughcast, down dazzling whitewash, ' wherever an
      elm arches,
Shivelights and shadowtackle in long ' lashes lace, lance,
      and pair.
Delightfully the bright wind boisterous ' ropes, wrestles, beats
      earth bare
Of yestertempest's creases; ' in pool and rutpeel parches
Squandering ooze to squeezed ' dough, crust, dust; stanches,
      starches
Squadroned masks and manmarks ' treadmire toil there
Footfretted in it. Million-fuelèd, ' nature's bonfire burns on.
But quench her bonniest, dearest ' to her, her clearest-selvèd
      spark
Man, how fast his firedint, ' his mark on mind, is gone!
Both are in an unfathomable, all is in an enormous dark
Drowned. O pity and indig ' nation! Manshape, that shone
Sheer off, disseveral, a star, ' death blots black out; nor mark
        Is any of him at all so stark
But vastness blurs and time ' beats level. Enough! the
      Resurrection,

A heart's-clarion! Away grief's gasping, ' joyless days, dejection.
          Across my foundering deck shone
A beacon, an eternal beam. ' Flesh fade, and mortal trash
Fall to the residuary worm; ' world's wildfire, leave but ash:
          In a flash, at a trumpet crash,
I am all at once what Christ is, ' since he was what I am, and
This Jack, joke, poor potsherd, ' patch, matchwood, immortal
          diamond,
               Is immortal diamond.

The great sea has set me in motion,
set me adrift,
moving me like a weed in a river.

The sky and the strong wind
have moved the spirit inside me
till I am carried away
trembling with joy.

I ask all blessings,
I ask them with reverence,
of my mother the earth,
of the sky, moon, and sun my father.
I am old age: the essence of life,
I am the source of all happiness.
All is peaceful, all in beauty,
all in harmony, all in joy.

GRATITUDE TO THE UNKNOWN INSTRUCTORS

What they undertook to do
They brought to pass;
All things hang like a drop of dew
Upon a blade of grass.

LAPIS LAZULI
(For Harry Clifton)

I have heard that hysterical women say
They are sick of the palette and fiddle-bow,
Of poets that are always gay,
For everybody knows or else should know
That if nothing drastic is done
Aeroplane and Zeppelin will come out,
Pitch like King Billy bomb-balls in
Until the town lie beaten flat.

All perform their tragic play,
There struts Hamlet, there is Lear,
That's Ophelia, that Cordelia;
Yet they, should the last scene be there,
The great stage curtain about to drop,
If worthy their prominent part in the play,
Do not break up their lines to weep.
They know that Hamlet and Lear are gay;
Gaiety transfiguring all that dread.
All men have aimed at, found and lost;
Black out; Heaven blazing into the head:
Tragedy wrought to its uttermost.
Though Hamlet rambles and Lear rages,
And all the drop-scenes drop at once
Upon a hundred thousand stages,
It cannot grow by an inch or an ounce.

On their own feet they came, or on shipboard,
Camel-back, horse-back, ass-back, mule-
            back,
Old civilisations put to the sword.
Then they and their wisdom went to rack:
No handiwork of Callimachus,
Who handled marble as if it were bronze,
Made draperies that seemed to rise
When sea-wind swept the corner, stands;
His long lamp chimney shaped like the stem
Of a slender palm, stood but a day;
All things fall and are built again
And those that build them again are gay.

Two Chinamen, behind them a third,
Are carved in Lapis Lazuli,
Over them flies a long-legged bird,
A symbol of longevity;
The third, doubtless a serving-man,
Carries a musical instrument.

Every discoloration of the stone,
Every accidental crack or dent,
Seems a water-course or an avalanche,
Or lofty slope where it still snows
Though doubtless plum or cherry-branch
Sweetens the little half-way house
Those Chinamen climb towards, and I
Delight to imagine them seated there;
There, on the mountain and the sky,
On all the tragic scene they stare.

One asks for mournful melodies;
Accomplished fingers begin to play.
Their eyes mid many wrinkles, their eyes,
Their ancient, glittering eyes, are gay.

In our souls everything
moves guided by a mysterious hand.
We know nothing of our own souls
that are unundertandable and say nothing.

The deepest words
of the wise man teach us
the same as the whistle of the wind when it blows
or the sound of the water when it is flowing.

Translated by Robert Bly

Between living and dreaming
there is a third thing.
Guess it.

Translated by Robert Bly

BUDDHA IN GLORY

Center of all centers, core of cores,
almond self-enclosed and growing sweet—
all this universe, to the furthest stars
and beyond them, is your flesh, your fruit.

Now you feel how nothing clings to you;
your vast shell reaches into endless space,
and there the rich, thick fluids rise and flow.
Illuminated in your infinite peace,

a billion stars go spinning through the night,
blazing high above your head.
But *in* you is the presence that
will be, when all the stars are dead.

Be ahead of all parting, as though it already were
behind you, like the winter that has just gone by.
For among these winters there is one so endlessly winter
that only by wintering through it will your heart survive.

Be forever dead in Eurydice—more gladly arise
into the seamless life proclaimed in your song.
Here, in the realm of decline, among momentary days,
be the crystal cup that shattered even as it rang.

Be—and yet know the great void where all things begin,
the infinite source of your own most intense vibration,
so that, this once, you may give it your perfect assent.

To all that is used-up, and to all the muffled and dumb
creatures in the world's full reserve, the unsayable sums,
joyfully add your*self*, and cancel the count.

As once the wingèd energy of delight
carried you over childhood's dark abysses,
now beyond your own life build the great
arch of unimagined bridges.

Wonders happen if we can succeed
in passing through the harshest danger;
but only in a bright and purely granted
achievement can we realize the wonder.

To work *with* Things in the indescribable
relationship is not too hard for us;
the pattern grows more intricate and subtle,
and being swept along is not enough.

Take your practiced powers and stretch them out
until they span the chasm between two
contradictions . . . For the god
wants to know himself in you.

We are the driving ones.
Ah, but the step of time:
think of it as a dream
in what forever remains.

All that is hurrying
soon will be over with;
only what lasts can bring
us to the truth.

Young men, don't put your trust
into the trials of flight,
into the hot and quick.

All things already rest:
darkness and morning light,
flower and book.

Call me to the one among your moments
that stands against you, ineluctably:
intimate as a dog's imploring glance
but, again, forever, turned away

when you think you've captured it at last.
What seems so far from you is most your own.
We are already free, and were dismissed
where we thought we soon would be at home.

Anxious, we keep longing for a foothold—
we, at times too young for what is old
and too old for what has never been;

doing justice only where we praise,
because we are the branch, the iron blade,
and sweet danger, ripening from within.

THE SEVENTH DUINO ELEGY

Not wooing, no longer shall wooing, voice that has outgrown it,
be the nature of your cry; but instead, you would cry out as
        purely as a bird
when the quickly ascending season lifts him up, nearly forgetting
that he is a suffering creature and not just a single heart
being flung into brightness, into the intimate skies. Just like him
you would be wooing, not any less purely—, so that, still
unseen, she would sense you, the silent lover in whom a reply
slowly awakens and, as she hears you, grows warm,—
the ardent companion to your own most daring emotion.

Oh and springtime would hold it—, everywhere it would echo
the song of annunciation. First the small
questioning notes intensified all around
by the sheltering silence of a pure, affirmative day.
Then up the stairs, up the stairway of calls, to the dreamed-of
temple of the future—; and then the trill, like a fountain
which, in its rising jet, already anticipates its fall
in a game of promises. . . . And still ahead: summer.
      Not only all the dawns of summer—, not only
how they change themselves into day and shine with beginning.
Not only the days, so tender around flowers and, above,
around the patterned treetops, so strong, so intense.
Not only the reverence of all these unfolded powers,
not only the pathways, not only the meadows at sunset,
not only, after a late storm, the deep-breathing freshness,
not only approaching sleep, and a premonition . . .

but also the nights! But also the lofty summer
nights, and the stars as well, the stars of the earth.
Oh to be dead at last and know them endlessly,
all the stars: for how, how could we ever forget them!

Look, I was calling for my lover. But not just *she*
would come . . . Out of their fragile graves
girls would arise and gather . . . For how could I limit
the call, once I called it? These unripe spirits keep seeking
the earth.—Children, one earthly Thing
truly experienced, even once, is enough for a lifetime.
Don't think that fate is more than the density of childhood;
how often you outdistanced the man you loved, breathing,
                    breathing
after the blissful chase, and passed on into freedom.

Truly being here is glorious. Even *you* knew it,
you girls who seemed to be lost, to go under—, in the filthiest
streets of the city, festering there, or wide open
for garbage. For each of you had an hour, or perhaps
not even an hour, a barely measurable time
between two moments—, when you were granted a sense
of being. Everything. Your veins flowed with being.
But we can so easily forget what our laughing neighbor
neither confirms nor envies. We want to display it,
to make it visible, though even the most visible happiness
can't reveal itself to us until we transform it, within.

Nowhere, Beloved, will world be but within us. Our life
passes in transformation. And the external
shrinks into less and less. Where once an enduring house was,

now a cerebral structure crosses our path, completely
belonging to the realm of concepts, as though it still stood in
            the brain.
Our age has built itself vast reservoirs of power,
formless as the straining energy that it wrests from the earth.
Temples are no longer known. It is we who secretly save up
these extravagances of the heart. Where one of them still survives,
a Thing that was formerly prayed to, worshipped, knelt before—
just as it is, it passes into the invisible world.
Many no longer perceive it, yet miss the chance
to build it *inside* themselves now, with pillars and statues: greater.

Each torpid turn of the world has such disinherited ones,
to whom neither the past belongs, nor yet what has nearly
            arrived.
For even the nearest moment is far from mankind. Though *we*
should not be confused by this, but strengthened in our task of
            preserving
the still-recognizable form.— This once *stood* among mankind,
in the midst of Fate the annihilator, in the midst
of Not-Knowing-Whither, it stood as if enduring, and bent
stars down to it from their safeguarded heavens. Angel,
to *you* I will show it, *there*! in your endless vision
it shall stand, now finally upright, rescued at last.
Pillars, pylons, the Sphinx, the striving thrust
of the cathedral, gray, from a fading or alien city.

Wasn't all this a miracle? Be astonished, Angel, for we
are this, O Great One; proclaim that we could achieve this,
            my breath
is too short for such praise. So, after all, we have not

failed to make use of these generous spaces, these
spaces of *ours*. (How frighteningly great they must be,
since thousands of years have not made them overflow with
        our feelings.)
But a tower was great, wasn't it? Oh Angel, it was—
even when placed beside you? Chartres was great—, and music
reached still higher and passed far beyond us. But even
a woman in love—, oh alone at night by her window. . . .
didn't she reach your knee—?

                  Don't think that I'm wooing.
Angel, and even if I were, you would not come. For my call
is always filled with departure; against such a powerful
current you cannot move. Like an outstretched arm
is my call. And its hand, held open and reaching up
to seize, remains in front of you, open
as if in defense and warning,
Ungraspable One, far above.

THE NINTH DUINO ELEGY

Why, if this interval of being can be spent serenely
in the form of a laurel, slightly darker than all
other green, with tiny waves on the edges
of every leaf (like the smile of a breeze)—: why then
have to be human—and, escaping from fate,
keep longing for fate? . . .

                  Oh *not* because happiness *exists*,
that too-hasty profit snatched from approaching loss.
Not out of curiosity, not as practice for the heart, which
would exist in the laurel too. . . . . .

But because *truly* being here is so much; because everything here
apparently needs us, this fleeting world, which in some
              strange way
keeps calling to us. Us, the most fleeting of all.
Once for each thing. Just once; no more. And we too,
just once. And never again. But to have been
this once, completely, even if only once:
to have been at one with the earth, seems beyond undoing.

And so we keep pressing on, trying to achieve it,
trying to hold it firmly in our simple hands,
in our overcrowded gaze, in our speechless heart.
Trying to become it.—Whom can we give it to? We would
hold on to it all, forever . . . Ah, but what can we take along
into that other realm? Not the art of looking,

which is learned so slowly, and nothing that happened here.
Nothing.
The sufferings, then. And, above all, the heaviness,
and the long experience of love,—just what is wholly
unsayable. But later, among the stars,
what good is it—*they* are *better* as they are: unsayable.
For when the traveler returns from the mountain-slopes into
the valley,
he brings, not a handful of earth, unsayable to others, but
instead
some word he has gained, some pure word, the yellow and blue
gentian. Perhaps we are *here* in order to say: house,
bridge, fountain, gate, pitcher, fruit-tree, window—
at most: column, tower. . . . But to *say* them, you must
understand,
oh to say them *more* intensely than the Things themselves
ever dreamed of existing. Isn't the secret intent
of this taciturn earth, when it forces lovers together,
that inside their boundless emotion all things may shudder
with joy?
Threshold: what it means for two lovers
to be wearing down, imperceptibly, the ancient threshold of
their door—
they too, after the many who came before them
and before those to come. . . . , lightly.

Here is the time for the *sayable*, *here* is its homeland.
Speak and bear witness. More than ever
the Things that we might experience are vanishing, for
what crowds them out and replaces them is an imageless act.
An act under a shell, which easily cracks open as soon as

the business inside outgrows it and seeks new limits.
Between the hammers our heart
endures, just as the tongue does
between the teeth and, despite that,
still is able to praise.

Praise this world to the angel, not the unsayable one,
you can't impress *him* with glorious emotion; in the universe
where he feels more powerfully, you are a novice. So show him
something simple which, formed over generations,
lives as our own, near our hand and within our gaze.
Tell him of Things. He will stand astonished; as *you* stood
by the rope-maker in Rome or the potter along the Nile.
Show him how happy a Thing can be, how innocent and ours,
how even lamenting grief purely decides to take form,
serves as a Thing, or dies into a Thing—, and blissfully
escapes far beyond the violin.—And these Things,
which live by perishing, know you are praising them; transient,
they look to us for deliverance: us, the most transient of all.
They want us to change them, utterly, in our invisible heart,
within—oh endlessly—within us! Whoever we may be at last.

Earth, isn't this what you want: to arise within us,
invisible? Isn't it your dream
to be wholly invisible someday?—O Earth: invisible!
What, if not transformation, is your urgent command?
Earth, my dearest, I will. Oh believe me, you no longer
need your springtimes to win me over—one of them,
ah, even one, is already too much for my blood.
Unspeakably I have belonged to you, from the first.

You were always right, and your holiest inspiration
is our intimate companion, Death.

Look, I am living. On what? Neither childhood nor future
grows any smaller. . . . . Superabundant being
wells up in my heart.

Ah, not to be cut off,
not through the slightest partition
shut out from the law of the stars.
The inner—what is it?
if not intensified sky,
hurled through with birds and deep
with the winds of homecoming.

Dove that ventured outside,   flying far from the dovecote:
housed and protected again,   one with the day, the night,
knows what serenity is,   for she has felt her wings
pass through all distance and fear   in the course of her
                                                                    wanderings.

The doves that remained at home,   never exposed to loss,
innocent and secure,   cannot know tenderness;
only the won-back heart   can ever be satisfied: free,
through all it has given up,   to rejoice in its mastery.

Being arches itself   over the vast abyss.
Ah the ball that we dared,   that we hurled into infinite space,
doesn't it fill our hands   differently with its return:
heavier by the weight   of where it has been.

Silent friend of many distances, feel
how your breath enlarges all of space.
Let your presence ring out like a bell
into the night. What feeds upon your face

grows mighty from the nourishment thus offered.
Move through transformation, out and in.
What is the deepest loss that you have suffered?
If drinking is bitter, change yourself to wine.

In this immeasurable darkness, be the power
that rounds your senses in their magic ring,
the sense of their mysterious encounter.

And if the earthly no longer knows your name,
whisper to the silent earth: I'm flowing.
To the flashing water say: I am.

Rose, oh pure contradiction, joy
of being No-one's sleep under so many
lids.

THE SNOW MAN

One must have a mind of winter
To regard the frost and the boughs
Of the pine-trees crusted with snow;

And have been cold a long time
To behold the junipers shagged with ice,
The spruces rough in the distant glitter

Of the January sun; and not to think
Of any misery in the sound of the wind,
In the sound of a few leaves,

Which is the sound of the land
Full of the same wind
That is blowing in the same bare place

For the listener, who listens in the snow,
And, nothing himself, beholds
Nothing that is not there and the nothing that is.

TO AN OLD PHILOSOPHER IN ROME

On the threshold of heaven, the figures in the street
Become the figures of heaven, the majestic movement
Of men growing small in the distances of space,
Singing, with smaller and still smaller sound,
Unintelligible absolution and an end—

The threshold, Rome, and that more merciful Rome
Beyond, the two alike in the make of the mind.
It is as if in a human dignity
Two parallels become one, a perspective, of which
Men are part both in the inch and in the mile.

How easily the blown banners change to wings . . .
Things dark on the horizons of perception,
Become accompaniments of fortune, but
Of the fortune of the spirit, beyond the eye,
Not of its sphere, and yet not far beyond,

The human end in the spirit's greatest reach,
The extreme of the known in the presence of the extreme
Of the unknown. The newsboys' muttering
Becomes another murmuring; the smell
Of medicine, a fragrantness not to be spoiled . . .

The bed, the books, the chair, the moving nuns,
The candle as it evades the sight, these are
The sources of happiness in the shape of Rome,

A shape within the ancient circles of shapes,
And these beneath the shadow of a shape

In a confusion on bed and books, a portent
On the chair, a moving transparence on the nuns,
A light on the candle tearing against the wick
To join a hovering excellence, to escape
From fire and be part only of that of which

Fire is the symbol: the celestial possible.
Speak to your pillow as if it was yourself.
Be orator but with an accurate tongue
And without eloquence, O, half-asleep,
Of the pity that is the memorial of this room,

So that we feel, in this illumined large,
The veritable small, so that each of us
Beholds himself in you, and hears his voice
In yours, master and commiserable man,
Intent on your particles of nether-do,

Your dozing in the depths of wakefulness,
In the warmth of your bed, at the edge of your chair, alive
Yet living in two worlds, impenitent
As to one, and, as to one, most penitent,
Impatient for the grandeur that you need

In so much misery; and yet finding it
Only in misery, the afflatus of ruin,
Profound poetry of the poor and of the dead,

As in the last drop of the deepest blood,
As it falls from the heart and lies there to be seen,

Even as the blood of an empire, it might be,
For a citizen of heaven though still of Rome.
It is poverty's speech that seeks us out the most.
It is older than the oldest speech of Rome.
This is the tragic accent of the scene.

And you—it is you that speak it, without speech,
The loftiest syllables among loftiest things,
The one invulnerable man among
Crude captains, the naked majesty, if you like,
Of bird-nest arches and of rain-stained-vaults.

The sounds drift in. The buildings are remembered.
The life of the city never lets go, nor do you
Ever want it to. It is part of the life in your room.
Its domes are the architecture of your bed.
The bells keep on repeating solemn names

In choruses and choirs of choruses,
Unwilling that mercy should be a mystery
Of silence, that any solitude of sense
Should give you more than their peculiar chords
And reverberations clinging to whisper still.

It is a kind of total grandeur at the end,
With every visible thing enlarged and yet
No more than a bed, a chair and moving nuns,

The immensest theatre, the pillared porch,
The book and candle in your ambered room,

Total grandeur of a total edifice,
Chosen by an inquisitor of structures
For himself. He stops upon this threshold,
As if the design of all his words takes form
And frame from thinking and is realized.

PAX

All that matters is to be at one with the living God
to be a creature in the house of the God of Life.

Like a cat asleep on a chair
at peace, in peace
and at one with the master of the house, with the mistress,
at home, at home in the house of the living,
sleeping on the hearth, and yawning before the fire.

Sleeping on the hearth of the living world
yawning at home before the fire of life
feeling the presence of the living God
like a great reassurance
a deep calm in the heart
a presence
as of the master sitting at the board
in his own and greater being,
in the house of life.

THE TREASURE

Mountains, a moment's earth-waves rising and hollowing; the
    earth too's an ephemerid; the stars—
Short-lived as grass the stars quicken in the nebula and dry in
    their summer, they spiral
Blind up space, scattered black seeds of a future; nothing lives
    long, the whole sky's
Recurrences tick the seconds of the hours of the ages of the gulf
    before birth, and the gulf
After death is like dated: to labor eighty years in a notch of
    eternity is nothing too tiresome,
Enormous repose after, enormous repose before, the flash of
    activity.
Surely you never have dreamed the incredible depths were
    prologue and epilogue merely
To the surface play in the sun, the instant of life, what is called
    life? I fancy
That silence is the thing, this noise a found word for it;
    interjection, a jump of the breath at that silence;
Stars burn, grass grows, men breathe: as a man finding treasure
    says "Ah!" but the treasure's the essence;
Before the man spoke it was there, and after he has spoken he
    gathers it, inexhaustible treasure.

BIOGRAPHICAL AND
BIBLIOGRAPHICAL NOTES

Angelus Silesius (1624–1677), pseudonym of Johannes Scheffler, German
poet and priest.

Bashō (1644–1694), pen name of Matsuo Bashō, Japanese poet.

Bashō gave this advice to his disciples: "Go to the pine if you want to
learn about the pine, or to the bamboo if you want to learn about the
bamboo. And in doing so, you must let go of your subjective preoccu-
pation with yourself. Otherwise you impose yourself on the object and
don't learn. Your poetry arises by itself when you and the object have be-
come one, when you have plunged deep enough into the object to see
something like a hidden light glimmering there. However well phrased
your poetry may be, if your feeling isn't natural—if you and the object
are separate—then your poetry isn't true poetry but merely your sub-
jective counterfeit."

See *A Zen Wave: Bashō's Haiku and Zen*, by Robert Aitken, Weather-
hill, 1978.

The Bhagavad Gita (5th?–2nd? century B.C.E.), the central text of the Hindu
religion.

"Those who realize true wisdom": IX.13–34, X.20. In this passage
Krishna, the embodiment of the Godhead, is speaking.

See *The Geeta*, put into English by Shri Purohit Swami, Faber & Faber,
1935, and *The Bhagavad Gita*, translated by Eknath Easwaran, Nilgiri
Press, 1985.

Bibi Hayati (?–1853), Persian mystic and poet; married to the head of one
of the Sufi orders, who encouraged her to write down her poems. She
also worked as a caretaker and cook for her Sufi brothers and sisters.

Blake, William (1757–1827), English visionary, poet, and artist; consid-
ered insane during his lifetime and neglected for nearly a century after-
ward.

"Men are admitted into Heaven," Blake wrote, "not because they have
curbed & govern'd their Passions or have No Passions, but because they
have Cultivated their Understandings."

See the wonderful contemporary account of him in *The Portable Blake*,
Viking, 1946, pp. 675ff. Henry Crabb Robinson, the diarist, a conven-

tional Englishman who met Blake several times, with a hilarious mixture of condescension, bafflement, and interest, said that "in the sweetness of his countenance and gentility of his manner he added an indescribable grace to his conversation," and described an early visit thus: "Everything in the room squalid and indicating poverty, except himself. And there was a natural gentility about him, and an insensibility to the seeming poverty, which quite removed the impression. Besides, his linen was quite clean, his hand white, and his air quite unembarrassed when he begged me to sit down as if he were in a palace." At one point Blake said to him, "I cannot think of death as more than the going out of one room into another." Elsewhere Crabb Robinson wrote, "I put the popular question to him, concerning the imputed Divinity of Jesus Christ. He answered: 'He is the only God'—but then he added—'And so am I and so are you.'"

The Book of Psalms (8th?–3rd? century B.C.E.).
Psalms 19 and 131 are traditionally ascribed to King David.
Psalm 104: This psalm has such striking affinities to the Hymn to the Aton by the pharaoh Amen-hotep IV (reigned c. 1380–1362 B.C.E.) that it may be considerably older than the above guess.

Bunan (1603–1676), Japanese Zen Master; worked as a gatekeeper until his forties.

Chuang-tzu (369?–286? B.C.E.), Chinese Taoist Master, philosopher, and comedian.
Probably the most famous passage in his book is the following: "Once Chuang-tzu dreamt that he was a butterfly, fluttering around, happy with himself and absolutely carefree. He didn't know he was Chuang-tzu. Suddenly he woke up: there he was in the flesh, unmistakably Chuang-tzu. But he didn't know if he was Chuang-tzu who had just dreamt that he was a butterfly, or a butterfly now dreaming that he was Chuang-tzu."
See *The Way of Chuang Tzu,* by Thomas Merton, New Directions, 1965, and *The Complete Works of Chuang Tzu,* translated by Burton Watson, Columbia University Press, 1968.

Dante Alighieri (1265–1321), Italian poet, universally acknowledged, with Homer and Shakespeare, as one of the supreme Western poets.
"This mountain of release is such that the": *Purgatorio* iv, 88–94. Virgil is speaking.
"The love of God, unutterable and perfect": *Purgatorio* xv, 67–75. Virgil is speaking.

"But you who are so happy here, tell me": *Paradiso* iii, 64–75, 79–87. Dante and Piccarda Donati are speaking.

Dickinson, Emily (1830–1886), American poet. She lived most of her life in her father's house in Amherst, eventually becoming a recluse and dressing only in white. The extent of her work wasn't discovered until after her death, when her sister found a small box containing 900 poems collected in packets (gatherings of four, five, or six sheets of folded stationery loosely held together by thread looped through them in the spine, at two points equidistant from the top and bottom). The total eventually came to 1,775. One hundred fifteen of them were first published in 1890, the rest in 1891, 1894, 1896, 1914, 1929, 1935, 1945, and 1955.

Her definition of a true poem: "If I feel physically as if the top of my head were taken off, I know that is poetry."

Dōgen Kigen (1200–1253), Japanese Zen Master, philosopher, poet, painter, founder of the Soto Zen school in Japan. His first religious experience occurred when he was seven years old, according to his earliest biographer: "At the loss of his beloved mother, his grief was intense. As he saw the incense-smoke ascending in the Takao temple, he recognized the transitoriness of all things. Thereby the desire for enlightenment was awakened in his heart." His most important work is the *Shobogenzo (Treasury of the True Dharma Eye)*, a collection of discourses and sermons in ninety-five fascicles, of which the central discourse is the profound and very beautiful "Genjokoan" ("Realization of the Primary Point"). Two brief excerpts:

> To study Buddhism is to study the self. To study the self is to forget the self. To forget the self is to be enlightened by all things. To be enlightened by all things is to drop off the mind-body of oneself and others. No trace of enlightenment remains, and this no-trace continues forever.

> Enlightenment is like the moon reflected in the water. The moon doesn't get wet; the water isn't broken. Although its light is wide and vast, the moon is reflected even in a puddle an inch long. The whole moon and the whole sky are reflected in a dewdrop on the grass.

See *Moon in a Dewdrop*, edited by Kazuaki Tanahashi, North Point Press, 1985, *How to Raise an Ox*, by Francis H. Cook, Center Publications, 1978, and *The Sound of Valley Streams*, by Francis H. Cook, State University of New York Press, 1989.

Francis of Assisi (1182–1226), Italian mystic, founder of the Franciscan order, and the most beloved saint in the Catholic Church. Known especially for his love of poverty and his fondness for animals.

Gensei (1623–1668), Japanese Buddhist monk of the Nichiren sect.

See *Grass Hill: Poems and Prose by the Japanese Monk Gensei*, translated by Burton Watson, Columbia University Press, 1983.

Ghalib (1797–1869), pen name of Mirza Asadullah Beg Khan, Indian poet of Turkish ancestry. His best poems were written in Urdu and are still widely sung.

See *Ghazals of Ghalib*, edited by Aijaz Ahmad, Columbia University Press, 1971.

Han-shan (fl. 627–649), Chinese Zen Master, hermit, and poet; his name means "Cold Mountain." According to tradition, he had a friend named Shih-tê who worked in the kitchen of a nearby Buddhist temple; Han-shan would come to the kitchen for leftovers, and the two friends would eat and laugh uproariously. They are often depicted, laughing together, in Chinese and Japanese paintings.

See *Riprap and Cold Mountain Poems*, by Gary Snyder, Four Seasons, 1965, and *Cold Mountain*, translated by Burton Watson, Columbia University Press, 1970.

Herbert, George (1593–1633), English priest and poet.

Hildegard of Bingen (1098–1179), German abbess, visionary, healer, painter, composer, preacher, and social critic.

Hopkins, Gerard Manley (1844–1889), English Roman Catholic priest and poet. His poetry wasn't published until 1918.

Issa (1763–1827), pen name of Kobayashi Issa, Japanese poet. Issa lost his mother at the age of three and was continually beaten by his stepmother; he later wrote that he "never went to bed without shedding tears." His later life was marked by poverty, prolonged family conflict, and the death of his first wife and four young children. But somehow he triumphed over all these obstacles and kept his simple, affectionate nature. He is particularly admired for his love of animals and his championing of the underdog.

Izumi, Shikibu (974–1034), court lady, said to be the greatest Japanese woman poet.

See *The Ink Dark Moon*, translated by Jane Hirshfield with Mariko Aratani, Scribner's, 1988.

Jeffers, Robinson (1887–1962), American poet.

Kabir (1440–1518), Indian mystic, poet, weaver, revered by both Hindus and Moslems; "Kabir" means "Great One" in Arabic. According to legend, when Kabir was a boy he recognized the Hindu sage Ramananda as his destined teacher, but knew that a Hindu wouldn't accept a Moslem as a disciple. He therefore hid on the steps of the Ganges where Ramananda used to bathe; coming down to the water, Ramananda stepped on him and cried out in surprise, "Ram! Ram!" (the name of the divine incarnation that he worshipped); Kabir then said that this constituted an initiation. Touched by his sincerity, Ramananda accepted him as a disciple.

Kabir spent most of his life in a tiny shop in one of the twisting alleyways of Benares. He was illiterate; his poems were passed on orally for generations, and are still sung by the common people all over India.

See *The Kabir Book*, translated by Robert Bly, Beacon Press, 1977.

Kūkai (774–835), Japanese abbot, scholar, calligrapher, founder of the Shingon (Tantric or Esoteric) school of Buddhism in Japan; also known by his posthumous name, Kōbō Daishi. He was the first Japanese to believe that in essence we are all enlightened and that everyone has the potential of attaining enlightenment in this very lifetime, regardless of social status, sex, or intelligence.

Lao-tzu (571?–? B.C.E.), Chinese Taoist Master, possibly legendary. According to the historian Ssu-ma Ch'ien (145?–89? B.C.E.): "Lao-tzu lived for a long time in the country of Chou, but seeing its decline he departed. When he reached the frontier, the guard said, 'Since you are going away, Sir, could you write a book to teach me the art of living?' Thereupon Lao-tzu wrote his book about the Tao, and departed."

See *Tao Te Ching*, A New English Version by Stephen Mitchell, Harper & Row, 1988.

Lawrence, D(avid) H(erbert) (1885–1930), English novelist, essayist, and poet.

Li Po (701–762), Chinese poet. Legend has it that he drowned after drunkenly leaning out of a boat to embrace the moon's reflection.

Machado, Antonio (1875–1939), Spanish poet and schoolteacher.

See *Times Alone: Selected Poems of Antonio Machado*, translated by Robert Bly, Wesleyan University Press, 1983.

Mechthild of Magdeburg (1210–1297), German visionary and poet. When she was twelve, she had a vision in which she saw "all things in God and God in all things." She joined the Beguine order of lay sisters in 1235, and led a life of charity, nursing, and strict religious exercises. An early Latin translation of her book, *The Flowing Light of the God-*

head, is said to have inspired Dante, and some critics identify her with the Matilda in *Purgatorio*, xxviii.

Mirabai (c. 1498–1546), mystic and poet, India's most famous medieval saint. A Rajput princess, married to the crown prince of Mewar, she refused to immolate herself on her husband's funeral pyre when he died. She flouted Hindu customs in many other ways; absorbed in her devotion to Krishna, she spent all her time at the temple, singing and dancing before his image, and mingling with the male devotees. Eventually, fed up with her family's harassment, she became a wandering ascetic. Her songs, like Kabir's, are still sung by the common people throughout India.

See *Mirabai Versions*, by Robert Bly, Red Ozier Press, 1980.

The Odes of Solomon (1st or 2nd century), a collection in Syriac discovered in 1909; scholars are unsure whether the original text (perhaps written in Greek) was Jewish with a Christian redaction, or Jewish-Christian, or Gnostic. The poem translated here is Ode 11.

P'ang Yün (c. 740–808), Chinese Zen Master, known as Layman P'ang. Upon his retirement in middle age, he gave away his house for use as a Buddhist temple, put all his money and possessions onto a boat in a nearby lake, and sank it. "Since his wealth was great," one ancient account says, "he worried about it. Once he had decided to give it away, he thought to himself, 'If I give it to other people, they may become as attached to it as I was. It is better to give it to the country of nothingness.'" After this, he and his wife, son, and daughter earned their living by making and selling bamboo utensils.

Layman P'ang's daughter, Ling-chao, was her father's equal in depth of insight. Here is one of several dialogues in which she has the upper hand:

> The Layman was sitting in his thatched cottage one day. "Difficult, difficult," he said; "like trying to scatter ten measures of sesame seed all over a tree." "Easy, easy," Mrs. P'ang said; "like touching your feet to the ground when you get out of bed." "Neither difficult nor easy," Ling-chao said; "on the hundred grasstips, the great Masters' meaning."

See *The Recorded Sayings of Layman P'ang*, translated by Ruth Fuller Sasaki, Yoshitaka Iriya, and Dana R. Fraser, Weatherhill, 1971, and *Original Teachings of Ch'an Buddhism*, by Chang Chung-yuan, Pantheon, 1969.

Rilke, Rainer Maria (1875–1926), German-language poet, widely acknowledged as the greatest poet of our century. The central event of his life occurred in 1912, when a voice spoke to him the beginning lines of the great *Duino Elegies*. Rilke had to wait until 1922 for their completion; in three weeks, caught up in "a hurricane of the spirit," as if taking dictation, often "in a single breathless obedience," he wrote down the last five Elegies, the fifty-four *Sonnets to Orpheus*, and additional poems and prose.

"Be ahead of all parting, as if it already were": *The Sonnets to Orpheus* II, 13.

"We are the driving ones": *The Sonnets to Orpheus* I, 22.

"Call me to the one among your moments": *The Sonnets to Orpheus* II, 23.

"Silent friend of many distances, feel": *The Sonnets to Orpheus* II, 29.

"Rose, O pure contradiction, joy": At Rilke's request, these lines were carved on his gravestone in the churchyard of Raron, Switzerland.

See *The Selected Poetry of Rainer Maria Rilke*, edited and translated by Stephen Mitchell, Random House, 1982, and *The Sonnets to Orpheus*, translated by Stephen Mitchell, Simon & Schuster, 1985.

Rumi, Jelaluddin (1207–1273), Sufi mystic and poet, born in what is now Afghanistan; founder of the Mevlevi, the ecstatic dancing order known in the West as the Whirling Dervishes. In 1244 he met the wandering dervish Shams al-Din ("the Sun of Religion") of Tabriz, an overwhelming experience that led Rumi into the depths of divine love.

Rumi's habits of composition were described by his beloved disciple Husam: "He never took a pen in hand. He would recite wherever he was: in the dervish college, at the Ilgin hot springs, in the Konya baths, in the vineyards. When he started, I would write, and I often found it hard to keep up with his words. Sometimes he would recite day and night for several days. At other times, he wouldn't compose for months. Once for a period of two years he didn't speak any poetry. As each volume was completed, I would read it back to him, so that he could revise it."

See *Open Secret*, versions by John Moyne and Coleman Barks, Threshold Books, 1984, *Unseen Rain, Quatrains of Rumi*, by John Moyne and Coleman Barks, Threshold Books, 1986, *We Are Three, New Rumi translations*, by Coleman Barks, Maypop Books, 1987, *These Branching Moments*, translated by John Moyne and Coleman Barks, Copper Beech Press, 1988, *This Longing, Poetry, Teaching Stories, and Letters of Rumi*, translated by Coleman Barks and John Moyne,

Threshold Books, 1988, and *When Grapes Turn to Wine*, versions by Robert Bly, Yellow Moon Press, 1986.

Ryōkan (1758–1831), Japanese Zen Master, hermit, calligrapher, and poet; his name means "Goodly Tolerance." Another Buddhist name that he took for himself means "Great Fool." Ryōkan is one of the most beloved figures in Japanese literature, and is especially known for his kindness and his love of children and animals; he even used to take the lice out of his robe, sun them on a piece of paper on the veranda, then carefully put them back into his robe. He used to smile continually, and people he visited felt "as if spring had come on a dark winter's day."

His most famous haiku was written after a thief had broken into his hut and stolen his few simple possessions:

> The thief left it behind:
> the moon
> at my window.

See *Ryōkan, Zen Poet-Monk of Japan*, translated by Burton Watson, Columbia University Press, 1977, and *One Robe, One Bowl: The Zen Poetry of Ryōkan*, translated by John Stevens, Weatherhill, 1977.

Seng-ts'an (?–606), Chinese Zen Master, the Third Founding Teacher of Zen. When he first met Hui-k'ê, the Second Founding Teacher, he said, "I beg you, Master, purify me of my sins." The Master said, "Bring me your sins, and I will purify you." After a long silence, Seng-ts'an said, "I have searched for my sins, but I can't find them anywhere." The Master said, "Then I have purified you." Upon hearing this, Seng-ts'an was enlightened.

The present version includes about half of the original poem.

Shakespeare, William (1564–1616), English actor, playwright, capitalist, poet.

"Be cheerful, sir": from *The Tempest*, IV.i.147–158. Prospero is speaking.

Stevens, Wallace (1879–1955), American lawyer, insurance executive, and poet.

Su Tung-p'o (1036–1101), Chinese civil servant, poet, calligrapher, and painter.

"The roaring waterfall": This poem was written under unusual circumstances: "At the Temple of the Ascending Dragon there was a famous Zen Master named Chang Tsung. Su Tung-p'o went to him and said, 'Please teach me the Buddha-Dharma and open up my ignorant eyes.' The Master, whom he had expected to be the very soul of compassion, began to shout at him. 'How dare you come here seeking the dead words of men! Why don't you open your ears to the living words of nature? I can't talk to someone who knows so much about Zen. Go away!' Su Tung-p'o staggered out of the room. What had the Master meant? What was the teaching that nature could give and men couldn't? Totally absorbed in this question, he mounted his horse and rode off. He had lost all sense of direction, so he let the horse find the way home. It led him on a path through the mountains. Suddenly he came upon a waterfall. The sound struck his ears. He understood. So this was what the Master meant! The whole world—and not only this world, but all possible worlds, all the most distant stars, the whole universe— was identical to himself. He got off his horse and bowed deeply, in the direction of the monastery."

For the complete story, see *Dropping Ashes on the Buddha: The Teaching of Zen Master Seung Sahn*, compiled and edited by Stephen Mitchell, Grove Press, 1976, p. 131.

Symeon the New Theologian (949–1022), Greek Orthodox abbot, theologian, and poet, born in Paphlagonia (northern Turkey). His discourses, which aimed at leading his monks into a greater awareness of God's presence within them, stirred up fierce opposition in the local archbishop and among the official theologians, and in 1009 he was exiled to a small town on the Asiatic shore of the Bosphorus, where he spent the rest of his life.

Traherne, Thomas (1637–1674), English priest and poet. The anonymous manuscripts of his *Poetical Works* and *Centuries of Meditation* were found in a bin of a London bookshop in 1895. After some skillful literary detective work by the editor and critic Bertram Dobell, the manuscripts were traced to Traherne, an obscure Anglican clergyman. When the poems were published in 1903, and the *Centuries* in 1908, they caused a literary sensation.

Tu Fu (712–770), civil servant, generally considered the greatest Chinese poet. He supposedly had such confidence in the healing power of his own poetry that he prescribed it for malarial fever.

Tung-shan Liang-chieh (807–869), Chinese Zen Master, founder of the Ts'ao-Tung (Soto) school of Zen.

"If you look for the truth outside yourself": "Just before leaving Zen

Master Yün-yen, Tung-shan asked, 'After you have died, what should I say if someone wants to know what you were like?' Yün-yen remained silent for a long time, then said, 'Just this person.' Tung-shan was puzzled. Yün-yen said, 'You must be very careful, since you are carrying this Great Matter.' Tung-Shan continued to muse about the Master's words. Later, as he was crossing a stream, he saw his own reflection in the water and suddenly understood what Yün-yen had meant. Thereupon he wrote this poem."

See *The Record of Tung-shan*, translated by William F. Powell, University of Hawaii Press, 1986, and *Original Teachings of Ch'an Buddhism*, by Chang Chung-yuan, Pantheon, 1969.

The Upanishads (8th?–5th? century B.C.E.), along with the Bhagavad Gita, the central texts of the Hindu religion. Traditional Indian scholars date them around 1500 B.C.E.

"The Golden God, the Self, the immortal Swan": Brihadaranyaka Upanishad, IV.3.12–22.

"Two birds, one of them mortal, the other immortal": Mundaka Upanishad, III.1.1–2.9.

See *The Ten Principal Upanishads*, put into English by W. B. Yeats and Shree Purohit Swami, Macmillan, 1937, and *The Upanishads*, translated by Eknath Easwaran, Nilgiri Press, 1987.

Uvavnuk (mid-19th–early 20th century), a Netsilik Eskimo. She became a shaman in one powerful moment: "One evening she had gone out to pee. It was a dark winter evening, and as she was pulling her pants back on, suddenly a ball of fire appeared in the sky. It hurtled down, directly toward the place where Uvavnuk sat. She wanted to run away, but before she could, the ball of fire hit her and entered her body. All her organs, everything inside her, began to glow. Uvavnuk ran back into the house, half unconscious, and began to sing. Immediately she was delirious with joy, and all the others in the house also were beyond themselves with joy, because their minds were being cleansed of everything that burdened them. They lifted up their arms and let go of all darkness, all suspicion and malice. The song allowed them to blow these forces away as if they were blowing a speck of dust from the palm of their hand. Ever since then, whenever she sings this song, she is able to heal others." (Adapted from *Intellectual Culture of the Iglulik Eskimos*, by Knud Rasmussen, Copenhagen, 1929.)

Whitman, Walt (1819–1892), American poet. Whitman's experience of spiritual awakening probably occurred in June 1853 or 1854 and shines through his first and by far his greatest poem, "Song of Myself." His deep compassion led him to work with hospitalized soldiers during the Civil War; he wrote letters for them, brought them food and money, fed them, and held their hands while they died.

"Trippers and askers surround me": "Song of Myself," 4–5.

"I have said that the soul is not more than the body": "Song of Myself," 48–50. (These are conflated texts: I have used primarily the 1855 edition, but a few lines that seemed to me improvements come from later editions.)

Wu-men Hui-k'ai (1183–1260), Chinese Zen Master, author of the famous koan textbook *Wu Men Kuan (The Gateless Barrier)*.

See *Zen Comments on the Mumonkan*, by Zenkei Shibayama, Harper & Row, 1974, and *Gateless Gate*, by Kōun Yamada, Center Publications, 1979.

Yeats, W(illiam) B(utler) (1865–1939), Anglo-Irish poet and playwright, generally acknowledged as the greatest English-language poet of the twentieth century.

Yeats's most powerful statement of spiritual truth occurs in "A Prayer for My Daughter":

> Considering that, all hatred driven hence,
> The soul recovers radical innocence
> And learns at last that it is self-delighting,
> Self-appeasing, self-affrighting,
> And that its own sweet will is Heaven's will.

A NOTE ON THE TRANSLATIONS

All translations and adaptations in this book are mine, unless otherwise indicated.

With the Hebrew, Greek, Latin, Italian, and German texts, I worked from the original languages. Sources for other versions are as follows:

The Upanishads: *The Principal Upanishads*, by S. Radhakrishnan, Allen & Unwin, 1953. I borrowed a good number of words and phrases from W. B. Yeats and Shree Purohit Swami, *The Ten Principal Upanishads*, Macmillan, 1937.

The Bhagavad Gita: *The Bhagavad Gita, an interlinear translation*, by Winthrop Sargeant, Doubleday, 1979.

The Odes of Solomon: *The Odes and Psalms of Solomon*, edited by Rendel Harris and Alphonse Mingana, Longmans, Green, 1920. I checked this with the Greek text of Bodmer Papyrus XI, discovered in 1955–1956.

Seng-ts'an: an unpublished literal translation by Robert F. Olson.

Su Tung-p'o: a literal version dictated to me in 1974 by Zen Master Seung Sahn.

Wu-men: an unpublished version by Robert Aitken Roshi, Diamond Sangha, n.d.

Layman P'ang, Tung-shan, Dōgen, Bunan, Ryōkan, Issa: all available versions in English and German.

Sources for Jane Hirshfield's versions:

Kūkai: *Tantric Poetry of Kūkai*, translated by Morgan Gibson and Hiroshi Murakami, White Pine Press, 1987.

Mechthild of Magdeburg: *The Revelations of Mechthild of Magdeburg*, by Lucy Menzies, Longmans, Green, 1953.

Mirabai: *The Devotional Poems of Mirabai*, translated by A. J. Alston, Motilal Banarsidass, 1980.

Ghalib: *Ghazals of Ghalib*, edited by Aijaz Ahmad, Columbia University Press, 1971.

Bibi Hayati: *Sufi Women*, by Dr. Javad Nurbakhsh, Khaniqahi Nimatullahi Publications, 1983.

The Milosz-Hass Kabir versions were translated from Czeslaw Milosz's Polish versions of Tagore's English versions of Kabir's Hindi.

ACKNOWLEDGMENTS

I would like to express my gratitude to the following bodhisattvas:

Richard Bartky, for the idea that initiated this book.

Michael Katz, my agent, and Jane Hirshfield, who were my generous collaborators at almost every stage of the editing, and treated me to ideas, poems, translations, tennis, tea.

Donald Sheehan, for alerting me to the passage from Symeon's Hymn 15, and for sending me the Greek text, a literal French translation, and his own, freer version, from which I have borrowed a number of lines and phrases.

Coleman Barks, for sending me several unpublished Rumi versions.

Robert Bly, Robert Hass, Czeslaw Milosz, Brother David Steindl-Rast, O.S.B., and John Tarrant Roshi, for their cooperation and suggestions.

David Bullen, again, for his excellent design.

And, as always, to Vicki.

ABOUT THE EDITOR

Stephen Mitchell was born in Brooklyn, New York, in 1943, and studied at Amherst, the University of Paris, and Yale. His previous books include *Dropping Ashes on the Buddha*, *The Selected Poetry of Rainer Maria Rilke*, Rilke's *Sonnets to Orpheus*, *The Book of Job*, and *Tao Te Ching*; his *Parables and Portraits* will be published by Harper & Row in February. He lives with his wife, Vicki Chang, an acupuncturist and healer, in Berkeley, California.